a study in time (and other lies)

Grey Gardner

Presentation by *BookLeaf Publishing*

Web: www.bookleafpub.com

E-mail: info@bookleafpub.com

ISBN: 9789357619165

First edition 2023

ACKNOWLEDGEMENT

To the incredible folks associated with the Inspired Word Cafe- both for being a wonderful audience and becoming some of my greatest friends and inspirations. You were the match to my growing flame. Thank you.

therapy drive

it's early October
my metallic beast is rumbling
over the asphalt
on my own,
I crave the purr of the engine
and the chance to hold onto the wheel
giving me certainty and control
which I lack in other areas

yesterday, I was missing
the shape of a friend next to me
rivalling my stick shift for a chance
to have my hand in theirs
today,
the moonlight illuminates
their profile
and the stars seem to hang low,
like one of those sweet tears
that touches their jawline

I can see it,
although my focus is on the road,
I catch their mind unwinding
in my blind spot

there is something simple about the therapy
drive
we're always headed somewhere but never quite
home

as long as we're okay,
there'll always be another exit
after this set of lights

34B

the very first time
I named the girls
it came in the form of boobs

boobs is an ugly word,
and as a poet I've never
been able to dance around
how ugly it sounds in synonym
landing more comfortably on
the ungraceful, tasteless "tits"
both the name of an alright bird
and straight to the point

not much to say
on those three letters
breast provokes images of cold cuts
in the frozen aisle at the grocery store
and tatas is just crude
and for what it's worth,
I can barely ascribe girls to them,
because I can barely ascribe that to myself
or can't at all
so that's it on tits, I suppose

In the fear of becoming
the poet that writes sexually
I have strayed away from talk of tits
and any other biological blackmail
I might have on my person

mutualism

I met a man who knew well how to rhyme,
whose writings rode on
natural iambic waves,
so impressive
for me to drown within his words

I'm all caught up
in the brewing storm behind my eyes,
squinting through them
trying to see
what he's so carefully crafted for me,
wordsmith of his own,
mirror reflection of my stories.

it strikes me that we have nothing in common
I don't write poems that rhyme or rhythm or
flow.
and I don't ask anyone anything
unprompted and reckless
as such.

ask me anything, he says,
like its the easiest thing in the world
ask anything
is open-ended at best

and yet it fills the silence in the room,
heavy and blue,
answers fuller and wider than the moon
eclipsed by my pride

what if tomorrow, we weren't here anymore
if death came through and held open the door
to whatever afterlife comes after this,
and death is waiting at the end of time
which we're reflexively wasting
at the expense of the other

and I want to prepare myself for his answer, and
I want to understand
and I want the
rhymes to wield something divine,
and more than anything,
I want to understand

my hairdresser died

my youth was framed
by virgin hair
its facade of purity and innocence
trailing lengths past my
delicate shoulders

its vines were carefully trimmed and pruned by
yours truly
until 20 years past their prime
my trust in myself waned
and I passed the shears along to her
I have always had a hard time trusting people
let alone people with full control over my
appearance.
after all
something so trivial could mean something so
drastic

it was sudden
a text
under the glow of the street lamp
on a Thursday,
she was gone
save for a memory from Wednesday
a warm light in her sunny Jeep

see you laters exchanged
for coffee

she was the first person to call me by name
and so had a bit of a hand in creating who I
would be
shedding the skin of a girl much younger than
me
to bring forth the metamorphosis
of a brightly coloured queer butterfly.

salon talk turned to impassioned rants
vulnerable monologues and
empathetic back and forth
and I can still hear her laugh
when nobody else is around
to entertain my one man stand up routine

hereditary

I remember wedding photos of my grandparents
framed in their home on fireplace mantles
gathering dust as the willow tree grew
its wandering hands meeting its steady roots
and I remember feeling small

my grandmother died after buying me a corsage
I still love red roses

I wonder what she'd think
about my life choices
post-mortem
how I drink coffee black
and always hated her fine china
and what a tragedy it was
that she never really knew me
what a shame it was that she died
just in time for me to love her

my grandmother wouldn't have given me more
time
would have said her death was a hard dead line
she was the maker of difficult decisions
for a Christian woman

I found she feared herself more than God
and I was sixteen
and feared misunderstanding her
just like I couldn't grasp religion
or politics

parabola

I've been describing my love
in percentages
perhaps making sense of something
logic won't encompass

mathematics was never my strong suit
and puzzles are often slow
drip like molasses through the recesses
of the mind
when I try to understand yours
your hand touching mine
side by side

I've been describing our love
in fractals
each piece artwork in a gallery
touching each other with a glance
across the hall
through the glass
I'd do it all
again just for you
formulaic and rehearsed
x meeting y
looks like me seeing you
through half lidded eyes
and glasses of wine

I feel you endlessly
through throes of time
you are perpetual and infinite
trustworthy in your certainty

my love,
I wish I could illustrate to you
just how exponential
you've made me

analog

three a.m. is my best friend.
I'm alone with myself and the world
and the darkness
and everything I'm familiar with is
enveloped in fairy lights
the gentle steady whirr
of the furnace
background to only my figure
silhouetted in the blue light
type.

my bedsheets are
one smothering away
from turning me ghostly
three a.m.
is the best time for writing poetry
because it's often the time
that stretches and distorts
the hour hand from the minute and

it's
four,
and I haven't written anything
and why is that?
I'm alone with the darkness

and even my mind has wandered away
leaving my body a desperate empty fleshy shell
and
who's to say I knew anything anyways
replanning my life
sorting my values in drawers
reset day after all

it is five,
and I'm making coffee,
and wondering what difference decaf will make
when the sun rises
if three was my best friend,
I can't rationalize why she left so quick
and I'm just as cold as I was
when I first laid myself to rest

permanent resident

I imagine they're married
and eat dinner together
it's a peculiar picture
they sit upon dining chairs
blissfully unaware
that I cried rivers
over that kitchen sink
when my second half didn't show
for the birthday dinner I made her
for the last year we'd be preteens
and what I unknowingly foreshadowed
in the spoons,
staring upside down at me
what would be the last year of our friendship

perhaps they were cutting the lawn
the day before I walked past
it was trim and neat and
missing the primroses
and there,
it pricks me.
		those were mine,
		this is mine.
and the thing is that it isn't,

and I am twenty, and
I still wonder why she never texted back
when she turned thirteen without me

I imagine their child
sits awake on the top flight of stairs
where the heat envelopes their feet
eavesdropping on their mothers too
if landlines still exist;
perhaps they write by quill and snail mail
in rejection of smart phones and television

I don't know what to believe,
or if I did,
I believe that they'll never be happy
in such a place that heaved such
heavy sighs and misery
and if I were to believe anything
I'd believe in the reality of the dust
and crumbling foundation
and fate that comes with
architecture,
fate that comes with soul,
house and home

message

I wish that I'd listened to you
I wanted to be someone
that much is true
I hate what I write
I don't matter to anyone else
I spent every day angry that I don't think
I could write if I tried even if
I stopped lying to myself
you inspire everyone
you're a good poet
even if you can't see it
until you proof read it
outloud and backwards

time and its punishments

I love you
is sewing my heart back together
fleshy parts that once were bloody
turned blush;
I always thought scars
were kind of cool
just like how I thought
laugh lines and crow's feet were a flex
on a good life well lived and lucky.
I love you after all
is accompanied by a show of teeth
and uncontrolled smiles
deepened palm lines
and under-eye shadows
are instead a job well done in I love you's
measured by practicing hands
and sleepless nights

high school soliloquy

dear beloved teenage queer,
first I wanna tell you sorry,
that despite it all I'm glad you're here
I'm sorry you're the odd one out,
The last to pick,
The third partner
Or the solo project
When people are scared of your courage
And don't understand your strength.

Dear my beloved transgender teen,
I'm sorry they choked you by suit & tie
Called you boy instead of queen
Mocked you at your high,
Took away your agency
In the attack on your agenda

I wanna tell you sorry,
That I wasn't there to draw my sword
Growl and snarl
and scare them off,
Keep you warm when you were cold,
Call you by your name.

Dear teenage queer,
Promise you'll find yourself
In all your friends
Misfits are everywhere
I promise we're just scared
Hope by opening my closet
You'd like to borrow my clothes
Baby sibling, I'd miss you if you go
Please hold on
For what it's like to hear your name for the first
time
said by someone you love
I promise baby
It's worth it all

Dear my beloved gender questioning kid,
I hope they learn to live and let live
You've always deserved better than this
I hope they show you kindness
And where love grows inside your heart
It grows back twice as thick.

enemy in the mirror

I am a prisoner
chained to a PDF document
in the glow of my own home
all alone all over again

I'm so tired
how are you?
how is it going?
and
the answer is
out before i think about it
it's
going
can't say well

I wish I would know my worth isn't word counts
that no rhythm or cadence will save me from
myself
that iambic pentameter was made up to haunt me
that rhyme and reason was made up to gouge me
when other work feels easier than my own
I am outclassed by even myself
can't write like I wrote yesterday

I didn't sleep last night because I was
too busy being on my grind
dreams don't work unless I
breathe. this isn't
working
it is two p.m. and I have
fallen asleep over my desktop
and gotten all too used to
being chained to a PDF
how long have I been here

no goodnights

I never hang up

I remember the last time I said good night
I kissed the phone and tucked it in
all in the name of beauty sleep
of making this love comfortable
albeit unconventionally

I never say good night.
It sounds too much like goodbye,
reminds me of standing on the patio
willing you not to walk away
your body attracted
by my lingering presence,
proposition, invitation,
door still open,

the rivalling temperatures of February air
and my heart warmer than ever within me
creating a balance that needs your indecision
to keep it even on the scale

stay, and keep it even.
stay
stay
stay

saboteur / creationist

I'm well trained in the art of giving up
other people call this clinical depression
I have been calling it artistic intent.

I'm creating life in my room
inspired by Mary Shelley
parts of me are recycled in places,
reused in others and replaced by choice
there's something beautiful in something
intentional
even if it's ugly the first hundred times.

art is anything I want and I stole it all,
I'm the great creator of my own destiny so I
ruined it
I'm Dr. Frankenstein and clinical depression is
my monster
Undefined and undiagnosed
wandering on his lonesome
wishing he could be something to someone
a great tragedy really,
to be human but not to most.
I'm well trained in the art of giving up
but I walk in the circle I've made for myself,
memorized by the earth to show me the way

to wait at the gates

do you ever think about what kind of cocktails
they're going to serve in the afterlife
truly if they have no consequence
they'll taste like no other.
we are waiting in line
for the greatest drink of all time
but what is the drink if not to chase death
what's the wine without the dry ache that comes
with
a martini is nothing without the control on your
own mortality
do I really want God as a bartender
He probably makes shit drinks
honestly,
what does God know about being alive?

morning ritual

you are starting again
water, grind,
dark roast today
yesterday doesn't matter anymore
except in what choice you have
in crafting yourself this delight.
how you take your coffee
is how you are as a person
and so what
if I'm born again every day
tomorrow, maybe I'm honey and cream
but today I'm espresso only
an ease that is familiar and not adventurous
tomorrow my taste will change
and I will choose my fate again,
just like I choose my proportion and roast
and start anew in process and wash.

I'll call you back

what is the phone call for,
if not to practice crying in silence
I'm personally proud
of my improvement with the skill
of making emotions a physical treat
a visual art and a performance

I was never a woman
because women are skilled actors
they cry on the inside
excellent performance
stage
presence
I see her hold onto the perfect wife,
she is shouldering the weight of her children
and they've never seen her cry

what is the phone call for,
if not for the practice
for when I admit I was never what I was shaped
to be
touched by society
what is the phone call to a woman
but a place to feel her emotions
without saving face

what's a sugar pill to a stimulant

there's nothing quite like it
life without the pill
wake up to music playing
same song from yesterday.
time is but a concept,
and you are floating down the river
with no sense of direction.
sunlight stopped meaning anything the minute
you stayed up late enough to see it inch up over
the horizon.

what about the pill makes you stay?
what about the pill makes it better?
the music stops
pause, silence, thoughts
forward
the day moves on like usual

there's nothing quite like it
I remember, the first time I heard my own
singing voice
thoughts clouded by no music, no arguing, no
debate
clear sky and melody.

evening approaches and its starting all over
no dosage adjustments prevent you from the
endless radio
people talking over me makes me want to rip my
hair out
like weeds,
and life without the pill
circles back once again
insomniac nights filled with your own light
that won't go
filled with music that won't stop
filled with ghosts that run their motor mouths
same as yesterday
same as always

I wish my friends would live

what they won't tell you about being gay
is all your suicidal friends you'll gain
you are thirteen years old the first time
they make you understand your own pain
in a mortal sort of way you never felt before

it would be one thing
to have one suicidal friend;
and at fourteen you don't even think its suspicious
to have two
after all you have two hands and all the love in your
heart

at your twentieth birthday, all you get is that you lost
count
you can't help but wonder who'd give you such a
disgusting gift.
and the hurt in your heart begins to ache in another
way
when you wonder which of your friends gender
dysphoria
is going to take first

dysphoria is a wild killer.
it has two guns in its belt pocket loops
and always draws first
when did you get this far without losing yourself
without losing them

consequence of which
was becoming one in the same at some point

me and my suicidal friends
scared and depressed in place
frozen and trembling with every news headline
holding us hostage
and we're tired.
you are thirteen years old the first time
that you hear a statistic on the wind
and have to pray its not a prophecy
and we're tired.
you are fourteen years old and
already wondering which of you
will give up first

you are twenty three
and people still call you she
without hesitating
you're writing poems,
and it occurs to you that nobody else fears their
friends dying
quite like you do
that nobody hesitates
when they can't take it anymore

god loves four leaf clovers

asking for you was
divinity I didn't know existed
ritual in its authenticity
and desperation
religious at its worst
luck at its best
prayer was always a gamble that way
a roll of the dice
cradled by my breath in my hands
how is it that you exist and God does not?
fate has proven otherwise,
luck has grown all over me
in the form of new spring blossoms
and you are every rainfall

goodbye

it is never sunrise
it was always the end of the world
even in the good places
the sunlight casting shadows
mirrored by prisms
bloody in all views
including the third person

I imagine that it starts with myself
the "I'm fine" of repetitive world ending
placing weight upon my psyche

I imagine that I'll meet you again
and ask you for the time
and wish for the familiarity of yesterday
instead you will say
       quarter to
and I will have wished I had died
instead of being forgotten

at the end of the world
nobody cares who you are
when there is nobody left to care

it is never sunset
I'm fine
when it starts again
nobody will tell me.